OUTside
INside
Poems

Voyager Books
Harcourt Brace & Company
San Diego   New York   London

OUTside INside Poems

by Arnold Adoff

Art by John Steptoe

Requests for permission to make copies of any part of the work should
be mailed to: Permissions Department, Harcourt Brace & Company,
6277 Sea Harbor Drive, Orlando, Florida 32887-6777.

Library of Congress Cataloging-in-Publication Data
Adoff, Arnold.
    OUTside INside poems/by Arnold Adoff; illustrated by John Steptoe.
      p.   cm.
    ISBN 0-15-200224-3
    1. Children's poetry, American.   I. Steptoe, John, 1950–   .
    II. Title.
    PS3551.D6609   1995
    811'.54 — dc20   94-25179

First Voyager Books edition 1995
A B C D E

Printed in Singapore

for
jaime levi adoff
and
the boys and girls
                    of
the yellow
        springs perry
                league
and
the little league
                pirates

OUTside

        the rain is falling fast like the falling curtain
      at the end of a school play
                     and the night sky is full of night winds
that
    bend the branches down
                on the old tree by
                     my bedroom window

OUTside

        the branches scrape the shutters of the window
        and
        the leaves brush against the glass panes
                   in the swishing rhythms
                  of the n i g h t rains

INside

      the house is my room   and inside the room is my bed
      and
inside
      the bed is
           me   under the covers
listening to the
   outside tree

INside

      my room   the light from the lamp
           that is shaped like
                    that famous
               duck
                      shines
        on my pillow
        and i smile

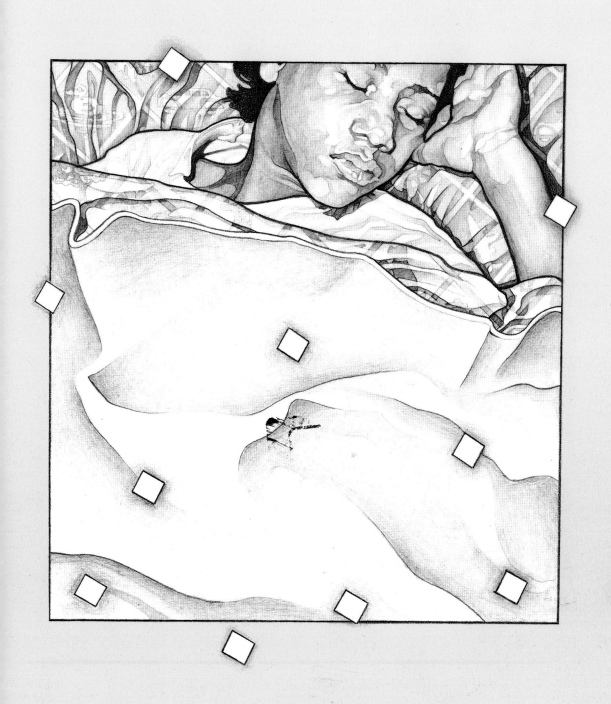

INside

     the light is shining through my eyes   into my hollow head
     and
        along a tunnel of purple paper
     to
     my   brain

INside

     my brain   the light of the lamp meets the noise of the bending tree
                           and the falling rain
       and light
        covers
        noise
          with a blanket of yellow
                clouds   and buttered pop
                       corn
                     lumps
   stuck together with brown sugar and morning dew

INside

       the longest second   and the shortest hour
       is
inside
       me
         and i am new

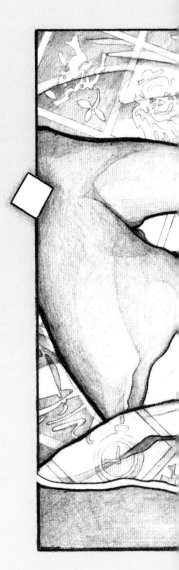

OUTside

        on the school yard field
                      i am standing in my baseball shoes
                       and yellow hat

                            that
                  new glove

        is hanging
               from my hand
                 and
i am just too
small for
everything i
       need to be a star

INside

       the baseball glove   is my hand
       and
inside
       the fingers of my hand
                are strands of golden wires
       sliding through
           my wrist bones   and up my arms
           to a secret
               central
               signal
               system
full of
flashing
       lights and creaking wheels and spinning dials

       all controlled by a green octopus
                eating
                    a

       peanut
       butter and tuna sandwich on toast
                while
                boasting
                  about

       his great
         games at first base
            at second
               base
           at third and
              home

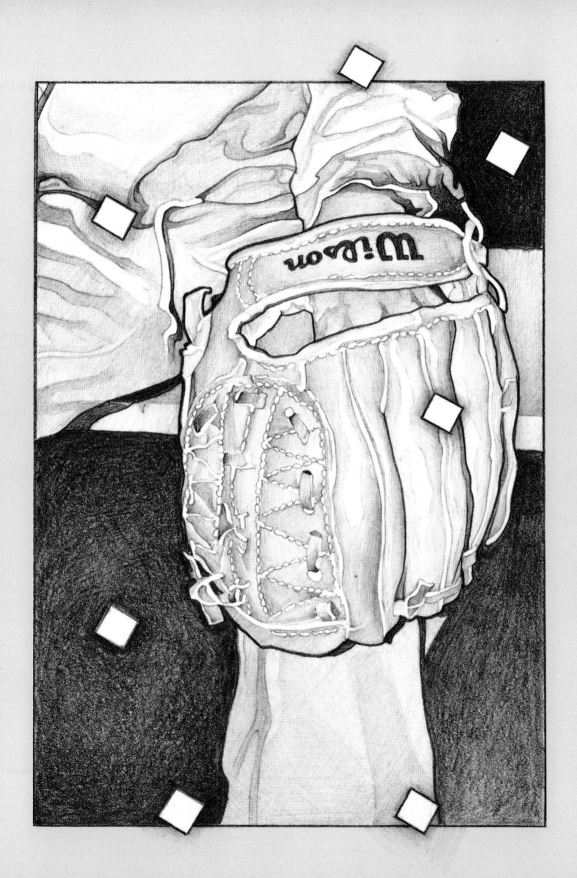

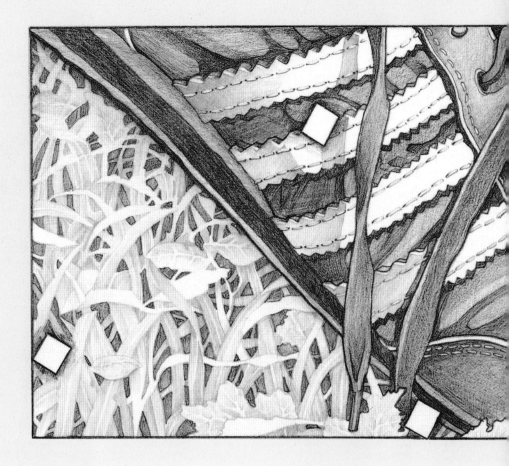

OUTside

        are the black shoes
                with the black laces
               that never stay tied
     and the scrapes
     on their sides
           from every slow
               slide

out
   side of every bag
  and into
      every tag

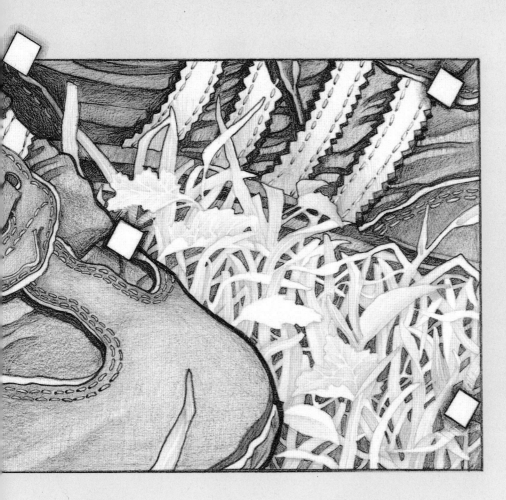

INside

       my shoes are green socks   and inside each sock
                                is a tan foot
                  and at the end of
                      each tan foot
are five unhappy toes

INside

    each toe is a bright red ribbon   leading through the ankle bones
                                 and beyond the bending knees to
                                 a central
                                     secret
                                     signal
                                     system

full of
flashing
          lights and spinning dials and whizzing wheels

          all controlled by identical
                              centipedes
                                   eating
peanut
butter and pickle sandwiches on toast
                                   while
boasting about
               team work team work team work team work team
                                                            work

OUTside

       i am standing at home plate   watching that fast ball
                          leave the pitcher$_s$
                                 hand
     and travel in a straight
                    line into the   catcher$_s$
                                 mitt
    while the umpire
    yells
        strike three

         three
out

INside

          and starting just behind my eyes
                                        the longest rubber bands
                                           s t r e t c h   out
          and travel through my head
                    and down my neck
                                   to meet the plastic ropes
                        that run up from my arms
          to a secret
                central
                signal
                system

full of
flashing
          lights and creaking wheels and spinning dials

          all controlled by a family of detroit tigers
                                        eating
          peanut
          butter and chopped liver sandwiches on toast
                                              while
                                              boasting
                                              about
                pouncing on the pitch
          or pouncing on the pitch_{er}

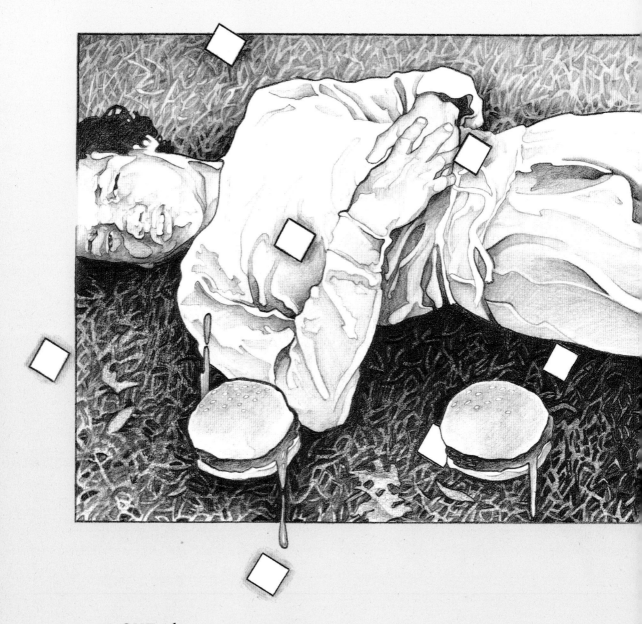

OUTside

       the ketchup and relish are dripping on my shirt
       in the middle
             of a hamburger
       in the middle of the team
               picnic

INside

      the thinnest silver circles
                          slide down my throat
and float across the river
                near my liver to a signal
                      system
                          so
                  central
                      and
                  secret
      where a grandfather rhino
                    is writing on the wall

N eaTnEss   iS All
        BUT IF u D rip don't
            S lip up
                on the
                ball

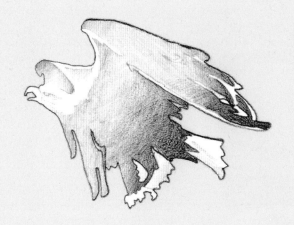

OUTside

      my pants are torn
      and there is a
              scrape
      on my knee

INside

      an eagle takes off
      from its nest
      and flies
           free

OUTside

the things that grow each day   keep growing into night
like my toe
                nails and head
                        hair   and fingers
and this
        best new
            set of teeth
                    that bite my good night snack
                            to disappearing

INside

       are the ribbons and wires   and the thinnest silver chain
       that slide and wind and connect

                          the fingers to the   brain
inside
       the story of a smile
             while
                base
                ball players sleep

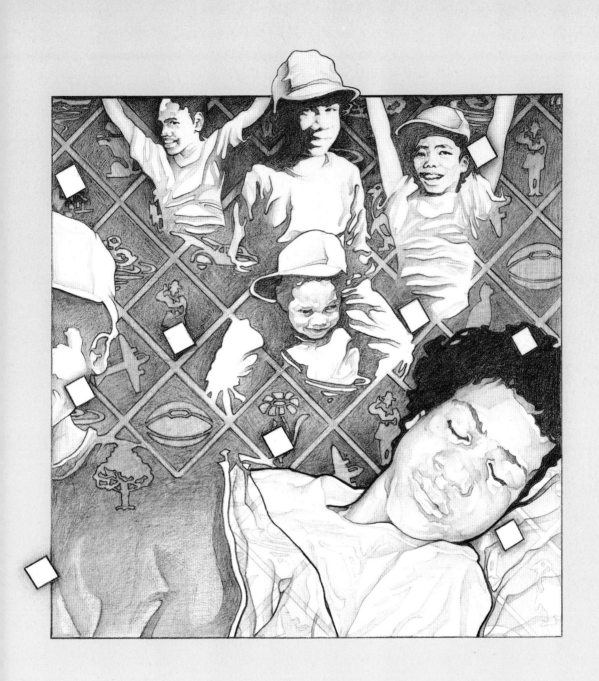

INside

       the falling rain   and the bending tree
     the longest second
              and the shortest
                     hour
    is
inside
    me
      and i am new

ARNOLD ADOFF, well-known author/poet/anthologist, was born and educated in New York City. He was a teacher and counselor in the New York City public schools for twelve years, and has taught at New York University and Connecticut College. Today, when not writing or editing, Arnold Adoff acts as a literary agent from his home in Yellow Springs, Ohio, where he lives with his wife, author Virginia Hamilton, and their two children. His book *Eats* was an ALA Notable Book, 1979.

JOHN STEPTOE wrote and illustrated seven of his own books for children, and received numerous honors and much acclaim for his work. He started working on his first book, *Stevie*, when he was sixteen. Published three years later, *Stevie* was an ALA Notable Book and received a gold medal from the Society of Illustrators.